For Whoever Thinks a Piano is Furniture

by Rudy Jon Tanner

edited by Deborah L. Fruchey

Last Laugh Productions
Walnut Creek
2023

ISBN: 979-8-9875209-1-8
Library of Congress Control Number: 2023902272

Cover Art: Peter H from Pixabay.com

Acknowledgements:
Many thanks to the generosity of Dr. David Kallinger, without whom this book might have languished in the "someday" pile forever.
And to Gary Tanner, for being kind enough to give me access to Rudy's unpublished writings.
Also thanks to Zeitgeist Press for permission to reprint Julia Vinograd's "Climbing Lightning", and to Richard Loranger for permission to print the obituary he and I wrote together.

www.lastlaughproductions.org

"Writing poetry is a relentless exercise in putting into language what is outside language."

— Leah Souffrant

"Every poem holds the unspeakable inside it. The unsayable...The thing that you can't really say because it's too complicated."

— Marie Howe

Table of Contents

"I hope you appreciate

the fact," she said, waving a limp, russet
azalea under my nose,
"That you're being gesticulated at
with genitalia!"

How I Answer the Phone

I'm sorry.
My answering machine is out for repairs
so the voice you hear is not only mine
but for the time being
human.
When you hear me sigh
please brace yourself for a live conversation.
Try not to feel nervous.

Busy Mind

Lots of things he didn't do
didn't eat the menu when he said he knew what he
        wanted
all that bone and flesh in the sea pitted against sirens
deep from his own belly, didn't eat
their words on the sleek page, mere hints
of sand bar breasts exposed in Venus shell, didn't
afford untampered crab, as usual, didn't even ask
for the menu, after all's said and done they're
                                        only words
skinny as the page itself when you trace finger and all
along the dotted line till you get to the English part:
the price

Didn't order anything but roast duck in noodle soup
and went on pouring aluminum tea
didn't pay attention to the mirror he sat next to
or cared what he looked like with chop sticks in
                                        right hand
and the *Odyssey* in the left
didn't ask himself at least this time
how many people here are seated alone
with book in hand, the left one, the one in olden days
we used to wipe with
but ate and maybe shook hands with the other

Didn't
think about those most previous times of filth
when they had perfume before they had bathwater
and didn't worry too much
that he'd forgotten to comb his hair though mirrors
have a way of reminding you
and in the course's end, he didn't
liken the double folded fortune cookie
to a mollusk or a Venus shell
or precious lockets of clam
exquisite bulbs of flesh less lasting

than portraits bosomed in miniature private, but I bet
there isn't anything private that can't be read, I bet
you could read shellfish innards like livers
I bet they did it. Didn't
pursue the thought, but wrote down anyhow
what he hadn't thought or likened it all to

Then found out for the first time
after how many roast duck in noodle
soups? You can eat the bones
you can eat the duck bones, they're cooked that soft
that's why they leave them in the meat
didn't figure that any such thoughts by themselves
could gain admittance to a Joyce's *Ulysses*
though he'd been reading out loud from the beast
all day, and though
"A genius is first of all master
of pettiness"
he mused
and wrote it down

as if there was such a thing as a muse
and not just Joyce with the pettiness
or anyone for that matter...at least Beethoven
had friends who would sneak in fresh
changes of underwear
"Where are muses like that when you need them?"
He lamented, but was intent rather on ending a poem
this one as a matter of fact
since he had started it before the soup came

and now was writing around the grease
spots on the skinny
paper cramped to the left as he had just gotten
to the "and now was writing around the
grease spots" part
cramped to the left of and by the shell of a bowl
with not even a spit left in it. And its saucered bones
too fat to swallow

as he broke the edible seal of fortune
and held over the bowl because he's never thought
there was a page that made good as a napkin
especially when what you're writing on is a napkin
and gave no further thought
as to how the poem should end, since
                                        he would discard it
along with the wise pearl in the sweet shell anyway

And for obvious reasons didn't complain too much
about why everything his busy brain writes
is disposable as any given napkin he may write it on
(never was a napkin that made a good page)
though this time it was "A Woman's Notebook"
he was scratching in, and true to its boast on the cover
"A Blank Book"
if quotes by women at the page top
make a book blank

A free, virtuous thing dredged out of the trash
"a find" you might say
fit for a bag lady
if her pen would know how to economize
what precious blankness there was
between the darkly limned blossoms
                                        boldly circumscribed
by some gentle, decapitating Ms
whose marksmanship for flowers he had
                                        found a soul mate in
when all of a sudden he hadn't forgotten

that this after all, was "Bloom's Day"
the day we celebrate Joyce
in all his elevated pettiness and on that note he
didn't leave less or more than 20% tip
the usual bone not for him
but for him, too fat to swallow
then commenced to perform cesarean
on the fortune cookie

that irrational pod we allow ourselves
to take in and be taken in by
let's face it, it isn't for tastiness
we break into that comma shaped trophy
horse neck smooth in the curve
curiosity and all the augurs of Troy is what they serve
like I say, the things we take in and are taken in by
on top of the facedown bill

But who doesn't
go ahead and eat the damned thing besides?
And didn't leave it as he found it, himself
the cookie's fragile shell
common blond as a wooden horse
but after curiosity strikes
more like a shattered piggy
bank with an I.O.U. in its belly
instead of a small fortune
and speaking of fortunes, didn't really "get it"
when it read:

> "Genius does what it must
> and talent does what it can."

but thought it kind of cute considering
before he had cracked his "just desserts"
he had just a few minutes ago written down
what first of all a genius is master of
and already had decided lacking in other material
to start there

Christmas Eve and a Ruckus at Clarksburg Mission

Down there
it's quiet as midnight mass
still running on the TV.
By now we've reduced the view
to a dead pan survival
the wispy sibilants
of the deaf.
It is not The Eucharist we stay awake for
with the milk and cookies left out.
Ignoring this, the image still diffuses
stonewalling our poker bids.
At this hour
everyone's a priest showing his hand
and turning the world to Muzak

In their own way
hands were beginning to show
down there. Raps coming in waves
against the walls
till voices rattled loose
and disembodied, *a capella.*
Now they dribble monotones.
Back where they left off, crickets fiddle,
folksing sidewalk crimes

The police are altar boys down there,
hands ready for the screen door—dog-eared
                                        and footswinging the peace
not that there was any ceremony to break
but they got the sneeze untickled in time
and all the wife wants down there
is no more fists.
Somehow pressed charges
is a fancy sound for more fists
so she lets him go and tonight
he gives her his distance.
She's holding her arms in her arms

a mime doing a madonna

He takes on the street lights one at a time
makes them fall behind single file
again and again the layers of his shadow
rise like newborn locomotives
but at least for tonight
there are no more fists.
Down there it's quiet as pillow tears
and they don't keep anyone up

There but for the Grace of God

1

I know we cannot tickle the downstairs screams
and turn them to fudge. To scrape free
the spatula with your teeth and tongue—
something your mother would call you inside for

Outside
the neon is free.
Inside, you do not push quarters
into the wall cracks if that nocturnal glow rinses
your window unblendably pink
or teases your fantasies
till you twist and twirl on skinny ribs
have you ever tried to untangle yourself
in a spinning drum? And the ceiling
the ceiling could be anywhere

2

Outside, they'll cap the scream hooded waves
with maraschino cherry beacons—soul
of circles saves and warns—for the life of me
I cannot make out the syllables
is it safe?
Can they call me inside for that?
Ru-dy...Rudy come ho-ome…
Is it punishment?
Is it reward?
The sweet meat at the door is
it could be either
and what Rudy Jon Tanner have you done
or rather not done
for it to be either?

And who uses my full name these days, anyway?
Beware of them!

Rudy Jon Tanner, You Come Here This Very Minute!
Isn't there something in there like a Zen koan?
THIS VERY MINUTE
you with the three name trinity
and the languid page-turning hand
without a mate
to turn the page back again
is it safe?
Inside where screaming is taboo, and sweet
evil flavors stay high on a shelf high
over your head
high?

3

Two every morning
every morning I tell you it's clockwork
a mad screamer passes outside below me
as if I were a turnpike built to stand crossing
over a turnpike
I can hear him with my window shut.
Never caught sight of him.

And blind the sun with my eyes!—is there insanity
without a Peeping Tom?
Does the late light on my window
pay for his passage?

You've stood under turmpikes, haven't you?
Heard the hum?
Did it ever turn into words for you?
To hell with answers, I'd settle for words.
I've thought of opening my window:
2 a.m., turn the tape recorder on
make out the syllables later.
To hell with words, I'd settle for syllables.
Push the rewind button
spin his trapped repetitions
no ceiling no floor, just turn

the page back at my leisure
hear the hand on the other side

4

Father Abraham, one drop
Just to cool my tongue
one drop   I know we cannot rinse away
a loneliness
in hell the ceiling could be anywhere
the window in hell being a one-way mirror
precious Abraham
how could there be a heaven for him
                    if he sees the damned?
And how could the damned be damned
if for one minute
they could take their eyes off of him?

Anyone regular as 2 a.m.
I don't care how skinny he laughs,
                    he would have the sense
to bum a cigarette wherever there's a stranger
like me
and suddenly it's English
good English
the button is pushed and playing

and I who don't smoke
so what do I know of ash, fire, sirens
passing hell on wheels?
All I know is, if ever I get called
outside
by name
like maybe this very minute
and this bum is waiting out there with his clear words
like maybe for a lousy smoke on his tongue
I'm going to want to dip my thumb in my own saliva
rub a slimy cross on his forehead
and hope to get that god damned mirror

smeared

Great Title Here
Great Author Here: Rudy Jon Tanner

This being the opening line, at least hooks curiosity.
Though what follows next is at best a vague notion.

But there is promise of poetic images to come.
Like
—in fact, exactly like
A window in front of a window.
Electric guitar piñatas.
A stack of angel wings...

All of which tantalize one with radiant hope
for development and continuity.

Like, for example, a stack of angel wings
ready to make up the skin

of a piñata shaped like an electric guitar as seen
from a window in front of a window!

And so taste is whetted for further development:

which happens in the form of lots of windows
in front of lots of windows
or electric guitar piñatas designed by
first of the instrument bashers, "The Doors"
or angel wings piled sky-high, all extracted
from left shoulders

(Parenthetically, angel wings are pressed one
shoulder at a time.
It lightens the load).

Not parenthetically,
but failing to avoid the superfluous, the
unnecessarily redundant

but at least succeeding at self-professed futility
not to mention what therefore won't be
mentioned here,
till sooner than expected we get all too close
to the approaching climax

with this line!

Which actually *was* the climax; this being
the anticlimax
which, not unlike fate, risks amusing only itself
in its tedious tendency
to dribble to the last *climatic* line, terminating with
overcast but no precipitation
though, of course, always open
for interpretation...

Pretend Children's Poems

In tribute to the classroom writing program, "Poetry in the Schools", poems written as a make-believe student in the program

Shoe Poem

I figured out
how to tie my
shoelaces today
but nobody was around.

What is Lucky?

Keys are lucky.
Think of all the peeking
they get to do!

If I were

if I were a floor
I'd stick out a nail
and kick back!

A Proverb

soap in a candy wrapper
doesn't make it candy.
I know.

Of Baby Fae and Her Baboon Heart

Stephanie Fae Beauclair (October 14, 1984 – November 15, 1984), better known as Baby Fae, was an American infant born in 1984 with hypoplastic left heart syndrome. She became the first infant subject of a xenotransplant procedure and first successful infant heart transplant, receiving the heart of a baboon. Though she died within a month of the procedure, she lived weeks longer than any previous recipient of a non-human heart.

—Wikipedia

I.

If you ask me I know nothing of baboons
if they turn and show me their red rears
it's so much baby rash to me

I don't know any more about hearts
if I was born dying
and no one's asking if there's anyone
who isn't
and they put a zipper up my chest
to stuff away the wang of that question
and the heart of an animal intercedes

the heart of Buddha as a hare
who leaped into the fire of a starving man
intercedes

because animals worship with their vitals
exposed
then you tell me who is animal?

I tell you it's musical chairs
with one too many red rears
what they do with the beat
and the interrupted music

and then the scramble primates know

so well—you tell that baboon
of yours I also know
what it's like to take your heart
and pass it hot potato on
before it cools mid-air in the hand
-to-hand combat
against being
rejected

you tell that baboon
(your baboon not mine)
we have enough in common
to be playmates

and while you're still on speaking terms
you might get it to tell me what I can do
(guilt pumping guilt
pumping)
if there is sacrifice here
feels like I am the one

someday I'll have to justify
every day I'll have to justify
every decision I make
mustn't let down
these extraordinary efforts of theirs
I did not request

and how do I share the too many riches
that borrowed time delivers
and wraps around these pathetic but tensile-
prehensile
fingers of mine?
It's what you ask the multi-millionaire
I mean how many steaks can you eat
off the hands of Jesus?

But if you asked my friend-twin baboon that
("Greater love hath no man than this,

that a man lay down his life for his friends…")
you'd be praying, wouldn't you?
Instead of dipping your fingers inside my chest
what do I know of fingers?

a baboon baby knows
knows how to grip belly and breasts
a man knows that
a surgeon
but fingers are so much sausage to me
wrapped in intestinal membrane
only wearing shiny instruments
like rings

best I can tell if they're not exposed
they're probably human
as if I had to tell you
the chest you ripple your fingers through
isn't that human

how did it get so full
this, my dead man's chest?
We're talking a baby's body here
mine
we're talking a very dangerous thing
a tiny
time fuse
a hot potato

we're talking innocence here
you've seen innocence
naked helpless
hideous
like in the divorce courts
something you win or lose
custody over

seen it pass from hand to hand
combat against being

rejected

we're talking one hell of a commodity
here
my dead man's chest
full of coins and jewels and death
and make-believe
death

let's
pretend X marks the spot
we'll dig here
it'll be fun
we'll be buccaneers together

a post-poned treasure in the sand
reopened

and you don't have to ask any baboon
I know my job alright
is just to be

put my faith in ambition
and let my precious
stones clear as pools
fuck the fingers that ladle them
your fingers not mine
what I call human

II.

On the life-support systems again.
I'm making my peace with God.

Yesterday a baboon came to me in my sleep
(I sleep a lot)
it had a misguided heart
I think it mistook me for a shaman

yes, shaman.
Or maybe someone's mother
anyone's mother—including my own
who, by the way, would have been less proud of me
had I taken more control over my life
like I say
anyone's mother

they all look alike to me
baboons and
mothers,
the masks of surgeons, and therefore,
surgeons
I haven't seen that many hearts to compare
but I have my suspicions

I couldn't tell if the primate was male
or female
genders look all the same to me!
Too many things look the same to me

take medicine
take faith healing
you have to be taught the difference, you know

the baboon and me:
We did not get introduced

some things you don't have to be taught
the difference. I recognize
the thorns
round heart-shaped cavity
deep in its chest
recognize the flame
you see in holy paintings hanging
around places like this

recognize
the saintly

finger   pointing
delicate unplucked petal that it is
                                        (Loves me / Loves me not)
that guides the eye down the cut-away
view of radiant cardiac flame
holy as Mother of God the flesh
or anyone's mother the flesh
is drawn like a drape and here
at last the crown
of thorns
I recognize

they wreathe around like knitted hands
of children
briars that ring—but where
is the fitting fisttight muscle?

the enchanted nut
the Sleeping Beauty
cradled tight in the briars—the home
of Brer Rabbit
                        tarbaby trapped
lying and cheating
the home of Buddha, the hare
rejecting on purpose the thistles and
trapped in the camp flame
trapped in the stomach
stomachs and briars, the castles
of any hare—they all look the same
hares themselves all
look the same to me

and I recognize precisely where I lie
my blanket printed with teddy bears
meaningless
all looking the same
I coil my identical fists
thumbs under
tender as fiddle-head palm shoots

coiled
tight as the core of Aztec corn
I recognize the enchanted nut

and see in the pupils of my nurses
(their eyes aren't developed, you know
but nascent enough to show me)
where I am holy to them and therefore
mistaken for anyone's mother

I am no shaman
but it's done without mirrors
the way I see myself

sleeping
invisible in my invisible
castle suspended
between the beats
they all look the same to me
castles
thorns
not the beats

each beat looks like a starving face
still holding on
to its dignity

the difference between medicine and faith healing
so I've been taught,
is dignity

I learned the difference yesterday
when Baboon profaned my sleep as if
it were the Sabbath
and blessed me
with the first choice of my life
(in my sleep I sleep a lot)
"It's my eyes, Doctor,"
I confessed to Baboon,

"I can't take them off the blind spot
my sight has pinned like a badge
to your proud chest
it isn't just any cave, Doctor,

it traps the light like a tarbaby
and it's getting awfully dark"

"Which would you rather I say:"
blasphemed Baboon,
"'Rise up and walk'
or
'Your sins are forgiven you' ?"
I think I scared it by not responding

this drove the Beast out of my sleep

I felt abandoned
I felt that also was a choice

What do I know of rejection?
What any adult knows
of rejection.
It's hard
to see a dead body and not recognize
how mistaken death is
about you.
To its sick eyes
(mistaken as anyone's mother) all living things
look the same

maybe you know something of baboons
how they all look the same
then you don't know about baboons
I don't know baboons
maybe my body knows something
about humans
how any victim mineral plant or
animal can be so human

appearances so undeceiving
till all humans begin to look
the same

don't ask me about rejection
ask my body better yet
ask my surgeon
he spare-changes for a living
keeps his hand out for hours
he knows about rejection

if I am to trust him
with baboon trust
at one point he has to discard
the patient as human
the victim as human
the fingers stabbed into your chest
as human
the fist yanked back like a fishing pole
more than in tact
as human
more than human
the still alive
remains flung to the temple steps
as human
less than human
downright animal

this I know something about
when you dance on your head
where the blood runs
                                        fragile
                                                    end up
digging
where X marks the spot
as to the Yogi, St. Peter
who refused to be equal

to his savior

in his crucifixion
fragile end up
as to a new born baby

in the hands of an angry god
slapping and inverting
as to your chosen body that zig-zags down
the holy steps
and hardens
I know something about bodies
made into stairs

and now that they think they've turned the temples
right side up
the pyramid base horizons the sun
oblique and wrong
the apex punctures the earth
absurd, impossible tooth
hollow as pit viper fang
and all the blood drains back
to the sun
where it belongs
all the robbed bodies wait like outfielders' mitts
shading their sick eyes
for flyball hearts
in the sun

and now that more than ever knowledge
is still knowledge
still sealed like memorized maps
in the skulls of priests
let the innocent and unwary

heart of an animal
intercede
exposed and alien
yours turning in
to mine
till every step that looks like every step

beneath it
is human

Break at a City Fountain

flute

oblivious praise

his breath
tunnels ebony

his voice clapping
heaven drains
to echo's
review
(his only encore)

blind improvisor!
(his notes
read by fingertip)
a Samson
between the columns
a hissing vacuum
in the side a psalm
for the cleansed
          recycled
          suspended

who
in the name of Job
tires
of this bright sound?

(perched
on a granite fountain
I hear the market's future
is in wormwood and pulp
and cellulose verses
gone metric)

perched
and standardized

clamorously never

catching their breath
the canon
of these Pan-ish pipes
remains

freezing the sanity level;
        impassable moats'
        sibilant music's
remains

Lost
        in order
                to continue to

piss
with precision
a circulation
more drinkable
than my own

according to the Archie Bunker Commentary, a reliable source

on looking back,
Lot's wife turned
to a *pillow* of salt
He's right.
She was remembering and keeping holy
The Seventh Day
back when The Lord, too tired to talk
after He had licked the alkaline sea
and so cultivated His taste for blood,
let Himself Out To Pasture
like a sacred cow, forever rambling
for something to rest His tongue

For Whoever Thinks a Piano Is Furniture

I.

On top of the lid closed level-tight
lest the angle of music uplifted
should wipe clean the tatted doily slate
on which porcelain angels play
porcelain harps.
That you cannot hear them
is the jubilee

What is genuine here?
Could you stuff genuine lilies down their throats?
I see them as planters for genuine fauna
their scalps punctured for the tiny stems
as though they were salt and pepper
indeed their hair should be turning
like maturing Chia pets
their hair watered and groomed
green, they should be nuzzled to fuzzy dos-a-dos
in mystical plant love
for long hair music

Imagine clapping hands
sandwiching a beat so *largo*
they measure the fish that got away.
Imagine patient braid of swinging partners
in a dance too slow to see

II.

How do you play, how do you *imagine* to play
with porcelain instruments that fan out stubborn
oxymoron solid bellows
against the squeeze?

Playing on the slick plateau of a Baldwin!

A Baldwin I don't have!
The black coffee table brags its vulgar expense
crafted to resemble
identically
a baby grand.

My god if you raised the piano lid
the earthquake!
The entire flat planet
lost!
It would expose the harp inside
the real one
the strong yet sensitive one.
Would that kind of shock warp it
from the unsealed environment?
The thing has a breathing inside!
ready to vibrate its mystical
oxymoron tense steel heart.

Let all heaven ski down
the dark stained stolid slope
along with the family portraits
all those braced smiles
their exposed ivory
all scooting into the abyss
of carpet—a smothering, toxic middle-class
cover.

Yet, better the bourgeois relics so defamed
than this room like steepled hands of children
should unfold itself to entertain
the "out comes all the people"
to itch unfolded chairs for a recital!
In the name of some household virginal
that this unearthly instrument actually get played
as upper and lower register
of ivory and ebony jaws open
to crispy stuffed celery hors d'oeuvres

And how could you negotiate escape hatch?
Jump in the belly of the beast like Harpo?
It would take shit-bang of a miracle
it would take elephant in the room taming of tusks
it would take the serving of scalding waterless
espresso
the sigh of steam ridden machines
the heart of automatons
keyboard calliope
a drill practiced over and over in
pretend escape of a merry-go-round

It would not take an encore
for ears well practiced
in sermon-still discipline.
No encore is going to politely stab the beast "to sleep"
and mercifully end the muffled, damper pedaled
bangs of glib technique
unless "encore" is a word *that* audience only knows
how to whisper on its lips.

Hugs

You let the chores hog them out of your life
till they get left out with the dirty dishes
and the left out ants who expose their necks
and bend their naked arms

By the hug they take up their chain of chores
and leave you in the kitchen alone
as though you haven't touched your food
and so have yet to be excused

What stays out too long will have to change
like cheese
cheese sacred cheese profane
whether on the floor or in the sky

Limburger or moon
left long enough, it dwindles to the dark
caravans of insects
or of stars

Where do they go, all the hugs we are too brave for
or too scared of, they all have to go
somewhere. All the hugs that were cocked and coiled
like embryos

In catacombs they dream of castles
in subterranean dreams they are carried off
by red or black armored
quests for sweets

The quick creeping knights
whose dropped reins drag the floor
blind as the tongue
to sally the unswept-away

That's what they are, the unhugged hugs
so many crumbs to be kissed and viced

in the horns of mandibles
mere dropped hints of our daily nutrients

So many backs
turned on the way out
like the grudge of moon—
that jaw of horns honed

sometimes by our own shadow
but from injury of its tenacious snub
and reflection of our own conceit, what shows of it
goes mistaken for the face

But of catacombs, who on the subway
couldn't use one? A hug, that is
a face, that is
I think it's the windows that do it

As if each other's eyes weren't enough reserve.
In our decline the windows get so dark
a danger of our own making lights up
the mere ricochet of seeing

What sees back
eyes
compound eyes
blind, underground insects that we are

Newsprint held in open and bent
well dressed arms
let us uncork the foam
and drink to this vile thing

To the hug, here, here
may we fill our transparent faces with champagne
then hurl our drained glasses at the black
unsooted windows

Bash glass against glass

till we can stare fixedly at the dark difference, if any
between what's been made to be seen through
and what's been made to be held

Mother My Bones

I dreamed we were in a class-
room writing notes to each
other. I could not read hers.
I could only read my own:

Mother my bones,

First of all my memories are too vague for me to
make love against their bodies. So try to relax.
So try to relax me. Perhaps after all it is time
we heard from each other. Though I prefer silence.
Would rather speak the way dolls and dogs speak
with children. Where the tricks remain unseen as
magic. And safe. Besides, I'm not likely to forget
the way you gave like the poor widow who with
her last mite made Jesus boast like a thief. The
way I took from you your right to beget. When I
broke your mould and you stopped flat. I was the
one, wasn't I, Mother? Who stuffed your mantle
with burnt pennies and sicked our leftover wishes
at the shooting stars? Lame for scapegoats—those
treetop lights. From their greed the cynical potbelly
night still grins at me its near-horizon
gold. An invitation wide as grandmother's wood-
burning stove door. So wide, Mother, that all that
remains is for us to be friends. We can even be
imaginary if you like.

Delivered upon waking, as
though it were a letter
opened and read aloud for
its recipient who cannot
read:

Perhaps it is my faith you would address. As patron of anonymous causes, I consider myself a descendant from that opportunist Fourth King who could not

decide which star would make history! The first
Christmas hangs advertisements on the sky. A
midnight sun? He squints through the fear of gazing
too long at his destination. A meteorite? Too
sane a glare to be taking potshots at the earth.
Comet? If so, it will pass...His faith in thieves
(that probably got him home) has returned in me.

But didn't you suspect all along? Isn't that why
you left me your mother's coin purse? I had just
come back from skywriting your miracles belly up—
the way you spent the last Christmas. But now
there were contents to pick: Love note hidden like
Jonah. IOU's backed up with your vomit. Lips
parted and gasping, rebellious as a lungfish, and
god I still can't believe this but inside, real
coins. Undigested as a Jesus parable. A little
queasy, I pry the trap jaws and with my finger gag
the black gullet that blossoms in needlepoint.
When out pour the alchemical poisons of silver
nickel copper and something neatly scribbled that's
been beaten to a white pulp. Mother, I learned
for a while to collect coins but I have never saved
goodbyes.

Pretend Children's Poems

Red Tailed Hawk

Red Tailed Hawk
from the film we saw
I know who you are.
how many sunsets
do you for free
get in to see?
Red Tailed Hawk
I see you
sitting in them

Zoo

snow leopard
you're not just plain
yellow
and spotted
and you know better
to dye your grey out.
you're panting now
but in the snow I bet
your coat is full
of golden suns

Frog

just by sitting there
Snap dragon frog
lets the rain
turn the flowers
into umbrellas.
as if he needed any!

Unnegotiable

On the street the night rain
resembled stamped leather vellum

Then changed to a dark computer card
behind which light escaped
through its holes, snagging
on constant changes.

As the downpour subsided,
the streetlight-reflected gutter cement
criss-crossed finely etched lines of light
as if light could stitch
fish scale sequins.

Under the night street lights
the skin of water, asphalt black,
tattooed in reflections
          and the dents of rain,
shimmers bead mosaics too abstract
                    and too brilliant
to set foot upon.

The Friendliest Message I Ever Got from AT&T

Model 5000 Answering Service Owner's Manual:

This answering service has a prerecorded
voice-synthesized
outgoing announcement.

This feature has been added for your convenience.
No longer do you have to think of the proper
words
to record

it's all done for you.

Your model 5000 automatically delivers
the following message:

"Hello,
the person you called
is unavailable
now.

Please leave
your message at the
tone."

We also understand that some of your friends
and relatives
may be initially reluctant to leave messages
without hearing your
voice
so we have included in the package
fifteen
pre-printed

postcards

that you may wish to send to those
people who are most likely
to call.

Noon Notes

Two brandy trumpets and a smart-aleck trombone hollering the breath of booze in the wind. And right now all over downtown San Francisco musicians are cutting off for themselves triangular islands from the street corners. On the eighth floor I can hear their evanescent noon hour euphemisms. They think they sound better than the street screamers. They think they can replace the beggars' blind lame blues, the homemade wood fife, the soprano recorder, and the Irish fiddle hooked up to his amp (The soprano recorder is teaching herself lessons. Publicly. She's on Book III, now, which she unashamedly paid for with exceedingly sympathetic donations). Eighth floor up I can hear the contrapuntal slurs of Imitation Dixieland over the IBM staccato.
It's noon. That means
There's a hot pretzel across the street. There's an awning full of tiny potted "ultra" violets (you'1l miss them if you're in a hurry). And on down the curb, black velvet draped card tables lay out flat shiny smooth metal jewelry. Ugly stuff. Sometimes a little turquoise thrown in. Little nuggets of nature in pentagram stars and moon horns.

Around the corner someone's voice box learned how the nose can make things carry. It is both broadcasting and droning the headlines—something about a chemical gas leak, a truck backed in too hard, the poison's free ride on the fog...the sentence runons are transported through tricklets of unkept saliva. The words somehow leak out and carry remarkably between and in spite of the tobacco spurts. Greasy overalled fat man and his papers. It's easier to picture him wrapping fish. But at least he reads the headlines. And maybe some signs. Probably out loud. On past to the next block a teenage girl is making the passers-by wish she could think up some verse for her two-pitched "Three Dollar Bags". Meanwhile brass instrument cases are laid flat open, set like traps to catch any derelict coins or wadded bills. They probably say to themselves, "if I had a nickel for every pair of hands clapping…"

Today a glass hauling truck cornered too fast over a manhole and spilled its complete load of mirrors. Big panel mirrors sharded to puzzling puddles of cloud and sky on the street, which was not so affectionately blocked off by the meter cop. She didn't have to trouble. The cars weren't willing to chance it. The pedestrians opened up a little. Small, predictable jokes. Something to share and exchange between the street curbs.

They said on the next street someone was yelling, "pocket mirrors, cheap!"

My mirror needs trimming & you're not here to do it

there are no direct ways for me to say it
the razor is a tongue
between steady teeth
the trance is smooth and creamy
this is not madness leavening my lips

that I meditate very clean
very painless
the edge barely perceptible
every day—barely perceptible
I meditate on things barely perceptible

I meditate on things that are supposed to be
dangerous for that reason
I meditate a fin
half lifts the surface
nearly mistaken for the cusp skimming

a wedge
fin
like hot blown glass swells a path
by dividing it
streamlines the foam

and then is overwhelmed
by honey smooth
Grave like a round stone
almost protruding
a brook—I swear I cannot tell

whether shark or dolphin, friend or
foe by that angular clue
and at this distance
both are indirect
both know how to circle

only by how much playfulness there is.
There are no direct ways for me to say it
let me say fear instead
it's easier that way
if there is outrage
enough you can shape and polish,
coast over my skin
as if only tested again
the untwining of every morning the same
duel with my reflection

we separate
permanent as harvest
and the one after that
and the next morning and the next morning
stubble eliminates the stubble
sun and fire to the dry stubble

and all I want to know is why wait
till harvest?
Whose appointed time is that sacred?
If you see him on the couch
what keeps you from waking him?

No. Something this resilient—blade of friend
blade of foe The Lord gives
The Lord takes the season away.
Isn't that enemy enough?
Where is the good in goodandevil?

Spring, an irrepressible
fencer: " 'Touché'," you say?
"We meet again tomorrow
same hot side same loam same gush."

And so you whet the edge
you haven't changed yet
each day takes longer

the same blade the same drain
neither of us keeps score

tomorrow you'll have to forget
what you took away today
Blade: "The bend of the rapier
is the test. How close can it reach itself?
Where does the brittleness begin?

Spring yields
the earth to hilt the grass"
(How balanced, how close
to the hilt, what I want to know).

DIVORCE THE KIDS
the teeter totter fulcrums

divorce the playfulness
(They're only kids).
No. First thing tomorrow
next stubble next fire
I'm going to bust up the glass
let the fire bell ring seven years

find out once and for all which one of me
has been doing the looking back
I'll mow the skin to honed sea shells
I'll find out how close the shard flays
next time

I steal grandfather's old Gillette
next time I try it without the blade
and this for me is the test
I've practiced at this, by the way
done it many times as a kid

only this time it's for real
I mean for the first time

as a man
remove the blade
if it feels like that
when it is loaded

that smooth
I mean that smooth
(slick commercial
throats proffered bare
as underdogs)

when it is so very very painless
I mean so extremely painless
just to get away
from that social event
of next morning's reflection

steady the war paint
the thick coat of dawn
the effulgent spill of dawn
the swift painless coast of sunlight
over the forest tips

Permanent. Blazing.
The stubble of dawn
bold and naked
as under dogs
routine but of all audacities
painless
that for me is the test
of the edge

there are no direct ways for me to say it
that by simply letting things be
placid, staring, no work no pay
a spoiled child in me stamps the circulation
back in my feet—those oblivious headstrong taxi
cabs

are supposed to take me somewhere!
Dammit, call out to them!
The hail bigger than Mary yields to a yawn.
Oh to catch one's feet in passing!
I am driven
to a mirror
shaving!

Shaving close
a balance of images and coast the tide
but a mirror has to hold still
it must not quiver if I fall into it
or I swallow my face whole
dissolve the clean deliberate paths
I've made round the jaws

I can still squeeze and stretch the skin a little
That's about it. Beat a path…
turn a fin or two upside down
a stabilizing rudder

ride it.
How does the surfer survive the fear?
His dangling feet could tickle squirming ribs
beneath him
jaws
fins
he knows how to catch a cab

start out flat on your stomach?
Guillotine meek lay down
your sternum like an ear to a railroad track?
How can you let something breathe like that
        beneath you?
The swelling dragon
of a love partner?
And paddle against the lull?
Then straddle the charge?

I'm asking you
how does anyone get up in the morning?
How?
Not just any morning but EVERY MORNING
How?
And with your lover next to you:
HOW?
How can anyone make a routine out of that?
Sure as the sun?
I tell you anyone who marries sure as the sun,
learns how to mate the sea.
And do it like clockwork!
Invert the fin

wicked in its size a tongue
a rudder for the feet
it steers
and balances
who needs it?
But this is how

I come full swing
the circles
our fingers taught each other
absent mindedly, almost accidentally
their trails that sometimes get swallowed
just above the hairline

just by letting things be
those games that barely surfaced
by no other means.
Playful.
As if they were never meant to be taught
or spoken

or even passed down
there are no direct ways for me
to say it

Commercial Between the Innings

Waves of human flesh the camera
waves back someone's eye
pressed to the glass
recording, transmitting
                                        beer
                                                        tilts on its axis
releases gold suns like healing balloons
some stars cling like ants
your eye presses to the glass
drinking and losing

Graffiti in University Psychology Building Bathroom

Did anyone here butt-fuck one of your friends as a
teenager?
Tell me all about it—how it happened and what
it was like.

Bob, is that you?

No, it's your mother, you goddamn son of a bitch.
And if you try to rub my clit one more time
when I'm asleep
I'll cook your fucking weenie for supper.

I knew it! It is you, Bob!

Shut the fuck up. I'm not coming for therapy
anymore.
I'll find someone else to talk to.
Some big help you've been

(1st Page, 1st Draft)
this work was never given any other title

How should you tell her you love her? Wait until the rain practices for you, practices up and down black key arpeggios which sounds like the keys are being cleaned on the hot corrugated tin roof down to where the gutter mulch backs up and not until it's ready will it leave, the rain, the easy rain, rain: the shelter you were born with.

It was just a warm-up act for what comes out sirens akimbo, translation: Flee to the cellar where you chat with the neighbors and catch up on the gossip and forget you fled to get there! Slams the rain against the wall, reads to the streaking street gullets the rights of the poor, reads no rights at all... this ain't no Mercedes you're driving wind at windows, this is no sun you're driving, sun slams the rain, comes out sirens akimbo, reads the rights to the rain slammed against a bank and pinned down where rainbows handcuff. Sun shakes down, tums itself upside down (If you ever looked, you'd notice). Sun rattles at the windows. Everyone unbolts, opens the door, opens the windows, turns off the security alarms, to patrol cop sun.

After the rain, you gladly let the sun grab your wet ankles, and turn you upside down, same as the rain shakes, sun shakes and rattles your blood to the head till you cough and gag through open jagged baby teeth. You'll have to cough up the pennies you swallowed in the rain, you a combination of hungry and curious wide as fledging mouth kid full of mulch backed up in the hands of a practical dad, you a hanged man flat as a card with stomach heaving to the spine. And when the pennies come out, why can't there just be pennies that come out?

Meanwhile and coincidentally, ankles still gripped in the clouds, you yourself start seeing like a little sun; you see the parade down below, a carpet of eyes looking 50 stories up, if eyes are antennas, if antennas hunger as much as eyes, if hunger gets in a long line. If hunger opens not the way you're opening! If hunger opens fledging gullets so one day when they too are old enough they'll turn upside down too and the hungry gutters will open beneath them and then no one will speak they will be so astonished that their gutter mouths can be that full.

When hunger opens, it's as if you're on security camera, as if always being watched. With hunger no one speaks openly unless everyday lie of hello-fineness is speaking openly. Don't tell her in all your hunger, hello you are fine, unless you mean it, and no one any one wants means it.

Wait till you are so hungry you mistake reflections for shadows. Rain or shine: heavy shadows. Then you're a child grateful for any tiny revelation. Look, the reflections myriad as rain, the photon-riddled dust hairs disappearing appearing like some marine language of suspicious lights behind the blinds opening and shutting. They are plaything baby bunnies come and gone, outgrown, the dust the rabbits and the spring rains, chocolate mud-clod eggs hoping if given enough heat to hatch into dry dust, Easter outgrown. Dust, the air, dust on every individual thing that has a krillion halo, dust, inertia materialized in light, particles not fascination to the outgrownups. Particles of no goal in no hurry.

They are like molecules they cleave to each other they choose to mate out of free will out of what we call free will. Each tiny crooked wiry tongue, when made visible by light, is a language of lights stringing molecular syntax in and out of the light like passing ships scared and blinking behind the window blinds a language of lights, born live like candles in opposite window across the street. Tiny tiny fire, flames very serious and still they laugh, it's the air current that makes them laugh, what we call free will. All the time the dust hairs laugh all the way down laughing giggling and that's what I call serious; that's even sad, especially the all-the-way-down part. Candles were meant to be lighthouse source steady, steady flex the fog muscle and same as sun and rain, both serious, both in the way, and fog muscles-in on pillar with a bright window at the top, same as any candle, that's the way they're built, built all the way down. And every fog droplet chooses, thinks it chooses out of free will, what we call free will, free in the company of droplets it chooses, not capable of thinking like fog it helps to make up which moves like an entity, like a school of fish, not inventing the current that makes it so choose, but mating and linking in molecular syntax the language of fog saying, "out of my way!" Says, "Confusion." Says it clearly. Says it with fog bellow flex of bay horns. Says it like a boast and saying it gives it away.

And you up there upside down hanging by your wet ankles in the clouds which is what we think we call flying. But flying in your own fog and trying to peek through to the surface fog like a world war spy, or like the free-will magnet of a boy's eye to a skeleton keyhole through a bathroom door, a fascination of light, the magnet no man can take away from eye. But takes away privacy which real boys and real men take away when they should be wondering about the name, "skeleton key," and why something has to resemble a skeleton before it can pass through the dust in the light to sitting nakedness of white freckled skin beneath what you've been calling mother and on into the masculine cuff to the head that can never, never take away the eye's memory which is like the sun's incapacity to do anything but choose to remember what it sees; it's the grownupness of the earth that blinks midst the language of lights and every night forgets it's been seen. If memory is the key of passing, if memory is the light and the dust and the bone and the came from, the mother, the just passing through.

High overhead at night you see what we call time on the surface when looking down, see lighthouse beams swing round, suggesting solid wheel of light suggesting what you see is a moon between earth and sea. See radar sweeps with trails you look in the hugging cloud at rotating star spikes and it's all done with mirrors the facade of rotating mirrors beveled and slanted toward horizon where light like sun born from sea is a mere facade of laughter all the way down choked in fog.

And you in your free choice slice through the air current push come to shove look down from your free will down there at a halo of rocks round the spinning wheel of light spokes where the rocks are baby teeth and the rocks are foaming and the rocks you know very well, you can't help but know there are always rocks between earth and sea there have to be rocks to cushion the blow a lighthouse and its rocks are a swing of old gate between earth and sea and this magic lantern movement the rocks this movement the things you are pushed away from the push come to shove shove of light, the push come to shove horn away.

They pile up—the things that are pushed away—pile up like dust. Light keeps piling up till you can see what's piling up. And the radar keeps piling up so you can see and fade away from what you see, so that the fear of crashing keeps piling up and the moon and moons everywhere pile up till the tides have to pile up and so do the waves pile up and the fear of crashing and the rocks pile up and the fear of crashing and the guano piles up and the island piles up and the birds pile up with their piled-up eggs like leftover warehoused chocolate Easter out in the sun till each chocolate egg melts from around its nut inside, which is called hatching, and the hatchlings pile up, trying to reduce their pile by reducing each other, and their failing piles up, and besides, the sea lions pile up and the shoving and the fighting and the barking piles up and they all every one are waiting in the pileup waiting for that push to shove moment to say I love you and vice versa and you have to take pause to ask how much hesitation piles up how much fear of crashing.

But if you take pause don't forget to do it with music, take pause, don't forget to negro the piano the black beat the beat the between the beat the syncopation the "Satchmo" rule: "If you can't tap your foot to it, it ain't music" foot accelerator pileup, the black pile of arpeggioed black keys piled up and sounding like they're getting wiped clean like I love you and vice versa that's when you take the dive-plunge of toe and hold on to sustain and pile up everything you play and all with your won't-let-go toe on accelerator gas pedal piano and know this is no baby's thermometer, your toe, no test of tepid bath, your toe is a ballet, a piled up ballet the notes remembered the toes counting like little butchered piggies remembering every time they get rubbed the notes remembered in the sustained and sustaining toe, and that's what gets played, the plunging bath you'll never forget cause it's only acid.

'Cause acid knows how to love you, loves your toe your foot tapping what's singing your head your flesh choked all the way down in your acid fog digesting bath and all the time you're wondering why there isn't more to love than this. And all the time you're wondering more and more why there isn't more and more till consumed to zero you say it you say the itching moment like absent limb you say I love you, I love you with rhyming dictionary I love you thesaurus in hand, in stump, I love you with guitar string so coiled, so unwrapped, so used to being wrapped around itself, so hidden and sealed in the new for so long it's decrepit. I'd love you with what would cut me in half if tried to string it out if it I ordered it up against the wall, if I searched guitar string for weapons if I ran my hands all the way down you don't have to be taught to run like that if you've ever learned to pat the neck you know there's no learning just remembering with strain at the neck your own neck with bulging tubes flushing bead in your neck and getting uncoiled and getting strung out in your neck and playing finger frets on your neck and tapping to the pulse I'd do it I'd love with strain with strain at the stool I'd vomit falsetto high as ungreased pulleys, love: I'd pull push grunt lift hang swing open, swing closed, swing upside down shadow like hawk silhouette to crazy untaught but definitely remembering chicks below, so scared of crashing so scared of turning into spokes of spinning stars and screaming their yellow light "run! There is something dense all around. There is something going to crash!" You don't have to be taught to run like that, bodies with heads cut off, their lighthouse bodies running around cause that's where they're going, and flapping their memories of flight till the air can't breathe for the feathers, and remembering mechanical-gear toy wound up and let loose and unwinding and free and running to prove it and that's what we call free will squeaking pulley wheels and gear wheels let go god the wheels and god the spokes and spikes and god what they cog-catch and turn of lighthouse night-day, of swallowed glass of light and pitch and mingled as flies and sweat and both iridescent and both attracting self-inflicted slaps and wings slapping and slap-slapping wings just to get beyond the smelly sunbeam, past the chicken trough past the post-hung harness and dust everywhere the close air the cough the choke that makes me wish for horse so long ago horse I wish for horse and the run I wish for what keeps farm alive is horse, I don't care what you've got the place died if it hasn't got horse, I long for wish for horse I bless the curved neck the guitar strings hanging down I pat you sugar you smell you hug you I hurl you like a rock like a guided missile I squeak I'm so scared of crashing I don't have to be taught, don't have to be taught dogs on gate's other side running mad with bark of seals we are here you are there but all the while tails wagging, dogs furious running, barking, all the time wagging they're having fun with I love you, I persecute you, I push to shove, I squeak if stepped on, you can't stop me I'm practiced, don't have to be taught, don't have to learn this "out of my way" 'cause now you understand me nice negro night when I say "clear a path" together we clear a path and if I spit my own puny spit of hurricane, that's me saying, "that's me," my push comes to shove l lubricate I squeak heavy wrought iron gate I love.

Dead Are the Boys Back Home

you and I know a dangerous place
don't blame me if I forget where

if you'd rather look at pictures:
cowed fire-eyes squint out the tears
squint out and out with palms hiding
cigarette tips

there is camp coned on the field
there are still-pictures taken
very still
don't blame me if I

forget where the danger is
that's what makes it so dangerous
it is easily forgotten

Pretend Children's Poems

Saturn

how did you know
the way I draw someone
with a hat?

Recipe

the only thing I know
that should go into
a good pie
is my teeth

Venetian Blinds

is that a suntan
or just dirt?

Unfinished

light bulb
right
    you try to rhyme it!

Dead End Alley

(for 1 voice, or Round for 2 voices)*

[1] catacomb eyes in a broken beer bottle
and a[2]cat on the rubicund tiles
horn of plenty in the shoe shine dew
and the work and the pay
gone dry[3], gone dry
and the work
and the pay
gone dry[4]

windows are out
and the dishes are out
of the windows
and the chandelier light bulbs
shattered in the shade
from a mattress mound
with the pillow-gut down
flying up like a chicken
on the bed spring piles[5]

catacomb eyes in a broken beer bottle
and a cat on the rubicund tiles[6]

**The rhythm of the poem as notated is actually a regimented representation of the normal rhythms resulting from the spoken words, and is practically what would result from reading it out loud without a conscious regard to a particular notation. Never-the-less, the indicated rhythm, especially with the Round version, must be strictly followed without the slightest deviation.*

1) In the Round version, VOICE 1 begins solo and is not joined by VOICE 2 until the word, "cat" is reached by VOICE 1, second time around (See notation for 2 VOICES)

2) In the Round version, VOICE 2 begins his/her reading of the poem with the opening syllable, "cat", as VOICE 1 reaches the word, "cat" on his/her second time around (See notation for 2 VOICES)

3) In the Round version, the poem ends for VOICE 2, second time around, on this word, "dry" (See notation for 2 VOICES)

4) In the Round version, the poem ends for VOICE 1, second time around, on this word, "dry." Hence, both voices end in unison with the words, "and the work and the pay gone dry" (See notation for 2 VOICES)

5) In the Round version, each voice upon reaching the word, "piles", returns to the beginning and continues without missing a beat (See notation for 2 VOICES)

6) End of poem for the single reading, which is read straight through as it appears.

1 VOICE

cata- comb eyes in a broken beer bottle

and a cat on the rubi- cund tiles

horn of plenty in the shoe shine dew

and the work and the pay

gone dry, gone dry

and the work

and the pay

gone dry

windows are out

and the dishes are out

of the windows

and the chandelier light bulbs

shattered in the shade

from a mat-tress mound

with the pillow-gut down

flying up like a chicken

on the bed spring piles

cata- comb eyes in a broken beer bottle

and a cat on the rubi- cund tiles

2 VOICES**
(ROUND)

etc. etc.

VOICE 1: cata- comb eyes...bed spring piles cata- comb eyes in a broken beer bottle
VOICE 2:

VOICE 1: and a cat on the rubi-cund tiles horn of plenty in the...
VOICE 2: cata- comb eyes in a broken beer bottle and a cat on the rubi- cund...

etc.

VOICE 1: ...bed spring piles catacomb eyes in a broken beer
VOICE 2: ...pillow gut down flying up like a chicken on the bed spring

VOICE 1: bottle and a cat on the rubi-cund...and the work and the pay gone dry gone
VOICE 2: piles catacomb eyes in a... horn of plenty in the shoe shine

VOICE 1: dry and the work and the pay gone dry!
VOICE 2: dew and the work and the pay gone dry!

** The rhythm for each voice in this Round version is the same as the notation for the single reading, with the indicated exception that each voice ends with his/her respective line: "and the work and the pay gone dry."

Embroidery

To watch the image form
sleep and writhe and stretch
as if it were the fabric
it is a weird fear
to trap the imagination
here emerging here stuffed
like spider eggs
the tinsel creatures low with silk
so fine that beauty weaves in it
and flies are spun

Felicity

I. THE JUDGEMENT

First time I abandoned a friend
I thought, "I will return"
and that settled it

I was relieved
I could now set my mind on other things

Like survival

After so many times of this
I decided to 'fess up and make my Second
Coming.
It never occurred to me if Christ couldn't pull it off
no way He would let me do any better

"Alright," I thought, "now to plot my return"
(I had not plotted my betrayal
I don't think you sit down and think, "now how
am I going to betray faithful ol' so-and-so?"
It comes natural)

Then there were more betrayals
more haunts and visitations in my sleep
aunts and parents and blood-brothers
letting me know
they were all dead now.
Nephews and nieces grew up behind my back
the little stabbers
it was getting out of hand

After years of no response from me
they all somehow met up with each other
formed a support group

from all parts of the country I received
letterhead mail from the national organization,
CURV
Coalition Uv Rudy Victims
(the E was silent)

As though from the bomb squad
as though my fingers were eggshell prayers
I opened each letter carefully
tediously
opened them all
with my handy Swiss Army knife that bears
insignia of cross on shield
it took every tool the knife could supply
including magnifying glass
(for finding clues and then burning the evidence)
bottle opener (for messages across the sea)
and for out and open assault: nail
file and tooth
pick

"Love is a many bladed thing," I thought
"you don't want to cut your thumb on it"

I'm not saying that when I love someone
I'm all thumbs
(though they can come in handy)
I'm saying the things I end up handling
they're an army of Swiss thumb nails, I tell you

And it was all junk mail to me, what they opened.
I swear if I read one I read them all
each letter consisted of the same one word
and the same punctuation:

RUDY exclamation mark

II. THE LONG TRIP BACK

"That settles it," I said
"I'm hitch-hiking first thing tomorrow
I'll meet them all head-on"
I felt relieved

bought a map
unfolded curves
                    and targets
                    that is, big cities
                    as circles within circles
which I suppose is good a way as any
to show ground zero

And for highways:
shields bearing numbers
                                        instead of crosses
numbers preceded by capital-I
and then there are the dotted lines
you shouldn't cross while passing
and are imaginary anyway

But that dotted line between any given
two states
it bothers me.
In the space between this dash
and that dash
between those dashes
do two states stop being
two states?
Blend?
If you tight-wire walk the border
could your foot slip through to trap an ankle?
Do you feel hot and cold spots under your soles?
Or are there invisible imaginary dotted lines
                    between
the visible imaginary dashes?

With even more invisible spaces
between the more visible though invisible dashes
ad infinitum?

Till nothing but maybe a microbe could
                                        squeeze through.
A rotifer maybe, with wheels for a mouth
and even then, if the land floods.
Maybe the smaller you get
the fewer the mental distinctions
between mental states

Maybe the smaller
the bigger loom other people's homes and gardens
intimidating as skyscrapers, all that property to
                                                            cross
just to reach the backs of friends and family
and then pass through.

Big job for a thumb so anonymous and tiny
it practically penetrates
by osmosis

and can't catch rides without staying open
and can't stay open
without losing a grip on the guilt and memories
which get so absorbed by the whizzing scenery
you even forget
who you've set out to see.

Happened to me
once I crossed the Mississippi
                        that boundary of filth equalized
and diffuse.
The land doesn't have doors it has borders.
Membranes.

I had to forget about having a place

to hitch-hike to
for Christmas.

If home is where the heart is
and the heart can be letter-opened
then sealed so you can't tell it's been gotten into
unless held to the light

And if the heart to a stranger is just
so much land
you have to pass through
and that's as open as it gets

What does that leave for a stranger to sew
from state to state?
Lands so vast and
private, the jokes they crack keep them
in imaginary stitches

You can tell by this kind of rambling
my sense of direction:
I lost myself in that map
through my Swiss Army
magnifying glass
staring so long and hard
till holes
burned
through

Which I suppose is good a way as any on the map
for showing ground zero.
And all the while my intentions got better and
better
which is what I could say for the newer and
speedier
wheels time drove by on

I suppose if you looked for details

from the air
you'd see an unfoldable map full of hot spots
but I didn't have to, where I was standing
wheels looked suspiciously round
small and anonymous
just trying to get through
stay alive
spinning and rolling smooth—that's the thing
that would impress a caveman if you dropped him
on a turnpike
before he'd get hit
how do they do it?
The wheels, I mean?
The god damned wheels?

But just like me
they rolled to a drummer all their own
spun out to their own little wars
left the road slicker than rainbows.
But unlike me
the only old friends
I ever saw a car leave behind

were shoes for one-legged bums.
The wake of every potential ride that whizzed by
me
fast as any scenery

absorbed the color right out of my flagging thumb.
With each buffet, a draft-stall-blast
hit me head-on
like a charging dotted line.
A wind spanking.

I'm not saying that when I repent
I'm all thumbs
but looking back, what was I thinking?
How could one pathetic hand appendage

have any better luck
than a Swiss Army knife
or the pen on this page, for that
matter

at returning me to any kind of a home
that could turn something as big
and impersonal as Christmas
into a place
worth writing home about?

Bomb

a lone
water blossom
dances to the breeze
the lure of wings
to the lure of battle
unfolding

Oppenheimer
the celestial bloom
robbed like honey
stung by the air

alone
the blossom blossoms
maddened
Oppenheimer hides

Guernica
April 26, 1937

infertile fields
scooped bone from the sky
like a heart in the hunter's
mouth

how could any living thing
yawn and keep down
so many flies?

Horsing Around

And I given some truth when horsing around
when last night when trying to make out I could
          tap dance
in the still sweaty not locked up yet ballet room
with just me and the mirrors
horsing around and damn near winning, too

there on the floor like wrestling wins when on top
and not on the floor ripped up like movie tickets
ever notice losing is what's gotta get flattened?
I've seen some lulus a couple hundred rubber
                                        necks
falling all over themselves just to get inside
some fine glob of concrete in order
to see Juan Gris' flat as a runover shoe
brand of horsing around.

And what the hay do they know not being
there and not being him except the bones
of there and him he turds behind
          the way you come across
left out unclampable suitcases or dead
t.v.s or some 1930s Underwood typewriter rusted
                                        up
out on the sidewalk you're supposed to trip over
so you'll think after you've busted your knee
you've really found something.

and here my hair's wet as a Sunday sailboat
feeling like I've been somewhere
last night and downright straddling my technique
the way I used to be able to improvise
on the piano if I could just sneak in
to a practice room and turn off the goddam light.
Hair dripping on the keys
it wasn't enough my hands had to sweat if I

imagined
I was doing it "for real"
by that I mean a live audience.

And I'd come out and a bunch of goddam
students
would be huddled around outside in the hall
sneaking their ears flat up to my door
same as me sneaking in there to begin with
see what I mean? About winning
and horsing around?
And what gets flattened? You tell me
which one of us had the flat ears?

And me, I had to quit music 'cause I couldn't
afford
to keep paying tuition and never could keep up
payments on a piano of my own
anyhow.

And I'm not bragging, you see, but I've seen
lulus I mean these guys could play anyone else
but I had chops and I mean chops playing my own
but being a perfectionist and all
it'd take me months to work up Kabolevsky
who wrote like an ungreased oil derrick
to begin with.

So guess which one of us had to go?
Thing is about horsing around and this is what
was given to me the other night when I was
what I call
thinking on my feet
with wall-to-wall mirrors echoing
just like a church

especially when everyone's filed out
after say Wednesday night Prayer Meeting

a time or two I'd sort of stick around for reasons
but a church that black
and empty is still full
of creaks and echoes you'd get awfully tired
trying to rationalize if it's horsing around
I mean really horsing around

I mean the kind that kept your cornered brain
guffawing
during the service in those stuffed as peppers
full of sweat church pews
well, you don't give beans about a Third Presence
if it's horsing around
it's just you and the mirror

which you see in the backs of who knows
how many heads
if you've cornered yourself in the right position
whether in the ballet room
or sitting in church
either case reflecting
backs of heads just itching
to get eggs broken over them

I'm not saying it isn't sad
when no one's there but your own reflections
all rubber necking to try to get in
I'm just saying what's so sad about it is
—and that's just the reason things so goddam flat

like sheet music and print and snap shots
and records and tape—recording and otherwise
and paint and ballet floors and unblowed-on sails
and mirrors
and railroaded pennies
and baseball bubblegum before you crammed it
in your mouth or later on got itself parasited
on your heel—both getting flatter all the time

and movie screens and the things that let you
in on them
and besides the movies you crowded into
to take lessons from
like a bunch of lulus, besides all that, there's your
own

lips flat on some lover's lips not thinking
my lips, how're they coming off
'cause my lips are a little too interested for that
right now
at the moment to be so interrupted

by the lighting
or by trying to figure out where does the third
person
come in—the sad thing about real horsing around
is this:
Who says the things that last are so
all fired up to begin with?
You flatten something out
you've killed the memory of it
the real guts

'cause the memory isn't the butterfly wings
you so tediously
racked out.
All that is, is just remembering
that something had a memory once
and I don't care how good it is, either
that's the only junk pile memory you're
ever going to pay
by the hordes good money
to get in to appreciate
like a square bunch of lulus
and speaking of that kind of money
maybe that's why I could never keep up
my payments

on that goddam piano

Haikuesque

pigeons drop their silhouettes
on the stained glass

ever ready for a poem
a pocket pencil
point nudges
my groin

a classmate fans her sweat
with my poems. a staple
improves the blank page

on twisted ends
two roaches tip my lunch.
since when are lovers
on time?

prints in window putty
balled in a bowl.
blue fingertips sealed
in the cold

a neighbor's anvil
is quiet between beats
of whitehot summer noon

My Body Hating Me and This Devil of Mine He

taught me how to turn
into a tree:
wear the Indian mask behind the
                                        cork carved live,
                                        the tree skin
                                        robbed for dance
not seal of wine

same devil taught me how to ride bulls.
"Hurricane" they said nobody could ride
                        it wasn't till the buzzer said different
that under me his loose skin got lost
I don't slide on blood
-slick muscle, I got my glove
roped to my fist.
ain't no other slack
under the strap round that branded
gristle and sawed off
horns of bell shaker.
I say:
if that's what I have to hold on to
                                give me a hand with the body
attached!

This buckskin hat I wear:
you think I treat it like shit.
I do
'cause when I ride, it knows how to fly.
and land.
and land filthy.
this devil says I can fly like that
(doesn't mention landing)
fly right through storm and it not even know it
if I want to
and I say, "you're on! I'll ride! I'll ride!"
only "I was just kidding," he says to me

"and you're gonna prove it," he says to me
and told me to stick out my tongue
as if I was makin' believe I didn't believe him
and he branded me then and there
right where it tastes
on dirt

It didn't burn much, my mouth wasn't dry
'cause no one told me I should have been scared
and that's why it took me all by surprise
he says, "looks like your time has come
for the makings of a tree"

"what, you talkin' camouflage?" I say.
but he carves on me some kind of initials
without the heart
"that's why the brand never hurt," I say to myself
"that's why I've been branding myself ever since
on the woodpulp page," I say to myself.

They say if it moves it's alive. I say
if you can skin it alive
it's alive.
and that's all the page is to me
just another thing alive. the page
this page
it's a flayable thing
a masking thing
and fibbing all over the place
a skin
on skin on skin and at the same time
if I have any say about it
never telling lies

each year the higher I stretch my never telling
the higher tattoos grow on me.
I want to get so high I can bend down
and read what's written without a heart

though maybe an arrow
but this here devil of mine he never taught me

how to read upside down
(though you'd think he'd know how)
or to read without a face
carved live with no anesthetic, cut
out of my side
for savage medicine
and dancing
and never taught me to ride

the girdle around
                    me
                        roped to a hand
                                or wait for the felling buzzer
just to get my nerves cut so I can't scream
though the cut teaches you how to fall
                                        out of everybody's way

and how do they give you enough time
to prepare to get carried out
with no slack between bark and chain wrapped
tight as my wrinkled skin
                                        still hanging on
                                        as if upright?

And who's keeping record
in the snow-filled tracks?
should be ready. After all,
there's no acting natural riding rodeo
and you don't radiate with other trees
if you're horizontal.

my chain drag ride is out of the forest
my ass is grass as a christmas tree
if there's any blaze of glory it's only
dead-end afterlife

                                        brightly bleeding time
in this slick snow I don't slide on blood

and the talk they do around me
        as everyone takes their own time now
sounds like funeral home ambulance talk
to me
has the rattle of no bell to it

believe I could ask what I've asked of clowns
and I don't mean pall bearers:
"Could use a little help around here!
Like a lift up?
Someone
        give me a hand
                                        with the body."

No Difference

Tonight there is no moon. Tonight like any other night—up there—there is a moon. There are crickets I can hear. And like the enemy in the bush, there are crickets I cannot hear. More of them than the others (though I can't prove that).

Aaron is my brother's nine year old son. Aaron steals a lot (though I can't prove that).
Aaron, your hands are pretending
you are hiding something!
You cup them over each other as if they were
freezing.

You peel open one stubborn thumb (all of Aaron's fingers and thumbs are stubborn). Like a sharpshooter, you close the eye you are not using, and hide the other eye in the hole of your hands.

It is a game. The pretending part is, that I am interested!

"What you got in there, Aaron?" I plead convincingly. He squints a pirate grin at me:

"You tell me," he chides wordlessly. A wrinkled nose enunciates it.

"Stallion?" I stab. For a split second Aaron peeks above his hands which by now have swollen into those horse hiding stacked boulders of old time Westerns. There is a white hat hero behind them now, using them to lightning rod the storm of bullets. As in the old Westerns, it's as if those bare, clumsy, socket fitting cliff rocks were the only things in sight that bled. Or could ever be hit. The hands Aaron steals with: the protection they provide is the only real target.

First Aaron bobs up to ascertain my direction of fire, then he ducks back down, docks his eye to compare the truth in his hands, with his memory of it.

"Stallion!" He snides, checking my truth with his memory of it. Down for another look. He'd be a sucker for peek shows. Up again, bewildered, suspicious, threatening:

"What kind?"

I once went to bed with my pajamas on—over my clothes. My mother kissed me goodnight. Then promptly withdrew the kiss. There is a humor gap between children and adults.

The same with poetry! A child replete with found poems may be yet to become a poet by adult standards. Though he or she starts out a poet by saying "Mine!" to everything. And possibly every child is a born artist. Though possibly not a good one. Word it as you like: All children are born liars. Though possibly not good ones. Aaron is no adult. But like a few adults, Aaron is an artist.
By that I mean
no one taught him
how to steal
an image while making it.

In that way, you might say all artists are sort of pack rats! Not excluding the life-style. His father knows his son has talent. His father doesn't know there should be no sophistication gap between Aaron's talent and Aaron's life. It was the same with me. The cat brings the master a decapitated mouse. The cat expects strokes and cat food. Doesn't get them. Not hardly!

There are two people in the liar-and-thief. One creates, one doesn't. You steal a flashlight, you're just Xeroxing. They find it under your bed: and Zap you're a screen writer! You say you got it from a bison headed Indian who was trying to prove telekinesis to you but can only work when you're alone. And in the dark... But you stick with it. And not only that you believe it. And all through the razor strap burns you're not begging. You didn't beg for the flashlight. You're not begging to keep it. And you're not going to beg for them to stop
your screams
and you're begging your screams to stop. And God help you, you still believe it, damn you. You'll believe it a hundred years from now. You're stronger than the tantrums of your parents.

Aaron is in danger of finding no respect—self or otherwise—outside his creative powers. Which means he has no means, if his father is too much like mine. We had lots of fun today, in spite of his grandfather's not wanting him to come in and out of the house. It uses up too much air conditioning. So we played outside. Wrestled and gave each other camel rides. I'm leaving in the morning. Aaron didn't mention it and neither did I. We put Aaron to bed, and though I'm not willing to prove it, we know he isn't sleeping—though he thinks he's fooled us. In time he'll learn better how to smother the sobs. It takes time. And I don't want to prove it.

Once it gets launched out of the trees the bruised moon withdraws and shrinks the higher it shoots. Though of course, the illusion is only in the cyclops eye of the beholder.

For the moon, so solitary by its distance above and beyond all depth perception, can only be viewed with a single eye. No matter how many eyes.

But sometimes the clouds show off, taking front-center stage with the spotlight for backdrop, scooting in and crowding out, playing

twisted, fascinating games. The play is so whimsical, yet so stubborn, there is no sophistication gap between the moon's talent and the moon's life.
The difference gets stolen more by each night.
As the moon gets stolen
more by each night.
Tonight, as it happens, there is no moon.
But nothing left to steal dissuades a thief:
Tonight, as it happens,
is like any other night.

Now that We've Separated

I will have nothing
I will have artificial ribs
I will have crushed crown of crab
I will have diamond corporations
beneath my fingers
between the keys
I will have red second hand clock
running the gamut
for a place to stick
I will have red salmon eggs on a fish hook
I will have correction strips
and mistakes made twice
the second, intentional
after being taught by the first
I will have shamrocks
collect them in pill bottles
I will have tiny plant freaks
pressed in my New Testament
I will have a scent
thread and hang
white blossoms under my arms

I will have my showers
in the morning fog
I will have the rain
sprout fine blond body hairs
I will have umbrellas
and high speed mushrooms
I will have trash
to empty
and then to refill
I will have nothing and feel myself
in the very best of company

The Mourners

They stand on tombstones
rigid, high and straight with no apparent
discomfort
they stand like statues with full
coats or overcoats buttoned
like unwrinkled monuments
in the cold they stand
as if they alone were the monuments and the
gravesites
were their pedestals
where indelible three-dimensional word and
image meet
to paralyze a memory
they stand stiffly with hands folded under arms
or under coats like tucked wings
with unfilled sleeves hanging
deadweight free
and loose
like amputees
or they stand with arms locked behind
their waists
or with hands slid deep
in outside pockets

they stand like pinball obstacles
there are no lights
no movements between them
the ground is unanimated flat
did someone tilt it horizontal
and freeze?
Was "Tilt" the only sun that showed?
Sun the number one god
one syllable god
is someone holding the land still?
That no stone rolls?
They stand like they don't know each other

they stand like they don't need to know each other

they stand as if their legs can't move
and were settled in their places by helicopter
as if they were plucked and placed
like transplanted chess pieces
like cutouts from various backgrounds
to be superimposed incongruously like Magritte
gentlemen with umbrellas they stand
above names

there happen to be on the face of one
smooth clean-cut right-angled
monolith
        Words Of A Name
Words of a Rank and Corps
                Numbers

above that name among other names
firm on the narrow top edge stand
three adults
stand as if homeless and proud of it
stand as if all year round they stay
unchanged by the elements
stand windless
one of them is a woman in double buttoned
                                        overcoat
and flats
ankles, shins and calves
exposed

behind her with arms around her waist
and gloved hands interlocked in front of her
stands a sailor with P-coat collar up
outlining sharply his chin and jaw
his white identification is pulled down
to straight across his brows
obscuring his head

to his left a man stands with every button
on his tan overcoat
buttoned
including upturned collar
the rim of his uptilted black felt hat hides
the crown
but frames his forehead with a dark nimbus
the three stand boldly
leaning in to each other
like heroes
huddled and elevated

they stand as if they were mannequins
carved out of the handles
of broad bladed spades
thrust partially into the earth
and waiting between shifts
they stand as if they belong there as if
they had blocks for roots
they stand as if they were proud models
for proud Norman Rockwell
they stand as if they believe
he still paints

they stand the way the dead sat
in the last act of "Our Town"
there are many of them
farther back a man straddles
between two of the white slabs
one foot on each
but not riding bareback stallions
in turn his own neck is straddled
by a child in white coat and hood
whose soft boots are anchored
by the man's hands
the child's hands
in white gloves palm both triangles
of the man's white shirt collar

this makes the man look like he is wearing
above his necktie
a superfluous white bow
the dark encircling
of the child's coat cuffs snug around his neck
look like strangling antennae
of a white butterfly
if the child's hands are wings

sharing the support of his left foot
stands stolid a dark haired woman
in dress, overcoat, and wide cuffed boots
in spite of the overcast a tiny cross
is reflecting below her neck
where she and half of the man are standing
there is only room for three feet
somehow it is clear the two lives sharing
the three footholds
are yoked
if her yoke is a light
chain and cross
the man wears his
by anchoring soft boots

there are others
so elevated
standing undisturbed
there is no breeze
perhaps there is music
there is no sun
and no color
their platforms are fine grain solid white

perhaps there is music
behind them all a small forest of maple trees
like arteries
ramify their stark limbs to make the sky a solid
vessel-gripped heart.

recursive, how a heart's beat ripples its own
vessels
there are no beats
and there are no vessels
visible

they stand in a clearing
and so they stand on manmade stumps:
upright blocks
if trees had no limbs I would say
they stand like trees
they stand like a training ground of telephone
poles
they stand like tall faces
of Easter Island
all face the same direction
many in front of many
on top of tombstones
trying to get a better view

perhaps there is music
or unison
firing of arms
an annual anonymous wounding
of sky

perhaps that is why they do not
speak
to each other
if what they are hearing
were not blanks
where would all the discharged
rifle rounds
land?
There are so many of them
each given its own particular
flight

like the sparrow "His" eye is on
father used to shoot sparrows
all year long
because of their droppings
shot them even in winter
in the naked branches
I am not so consoled if that is what
"His eye is on"
or that "He watches me".

Paint

Paint rides on the tails of horses
that web the wind
and make it shine

Pro Nuclear Energy Argument Number One

What's wrong with you is you don't weigh the
benefits. You gotta be willing to pay the
price. For example, did you know that without
World War II we never would have gotten the
electric toaster?
Hm?
Think about it !
The Electric Toaster!

We didn't let a little fission stop us then.

Pro Nuclear Energy Argument Number Two

I. You gotta admit. It is clean.

A. Every bit as clean as the paper
napkin this is written on, or any
other theoretical sponge convenience
will take by storm.

B. As any hurricane's eye would tell
you. It's even cleaner than the path
of a wet rag on a counter at Sambo's.

C. I mean poet that I am I've never
churned butter by placing a tiger
next to an ethnic stereotype but I bet
you it's slicker than that.

D. I bet you it is so clean you could
chase a nigger-baby for days on end
and never get your feet black. I mean
it just doesn't rub off like that
considering the momentum.

E. Consider the momentum! Atoms
infectiously mad as rabies hot on
each other's tail and the only thing
that rubs off is the breath of a planet
and who ever sees that anyway?
Whether it's melted down or spread
thin as chiffon?

II. I mean you gotta admit. You couldn't paper
train a hungry tiger on a disposable napkin and
expect to get any cleaner than that.

Pretend Children's Poems

Butterfly

Butterfly flits and flattens
then gets up and flits again.
Open close
glide, and land
very stupid butterfly!
Never thinks of flying in a straight line
as if there were no such thing
as the shortest distance to happiness

Dear stained glass window-wings:
if only you weren't a bug!
Everything about you is so beautiful
except for you!

Voodoo

Why chickens?
our hope in eggs
short-term or long-term?

Besides wings that incubate,
wings for emergencies only?
that chickens scatter easily
with no intent to escape?
a lesson for the Human Condition?

But likewise pigeons.
who brazenly feed on the Human Condition
in plain sight—the first requirement
for magic.

But is it that chickens are rural, closer
to earth and grain
and earth hides things
including roots?

Is it that chickens are so stupid
or brilliant
to think every single dawn
is worth shouting about?
magic enough for me!

Or is it that you cannot educate
a chicken but decapitation
puts both feet and wings into action?

Is it that cocks in a betting ring
each decide about the other
without coaxing
and so prove the absence
of Free Will?

Maybe voodoo is an exotic word
for our hypnotism
(as if in all our learnedness
we could explain that
any better).

Or
is it
that each cock's knowledge
of subjecting one's will
to the will of another
is something we all understand?
requiring no education?
But all species know of this
and teach it
as further proof all around us

Every Single Day
for the sake of the stubborn, no doubt
and the blind who can't see the
invisible tricks
about Free Will.

If there is universal appeal
for power without education
is there also a universal catch?
call it magic
or mafia?

Chickens may be magical because you don't have
to be a magician
to put a spell on a chicken:

draw a line on the ground
grab the chicken's head
and touch its beak to the line.
Why on Earth
does that hypnotize

the chicken?

Maybe chickens are sacred to voodoo
because no spell exists
that can protect anyone
from becoming inanimate
mid-peck.

On Oxymorons and Profundity

Avoid oxymorons.*

If all poets followed this simple rule tv would be a thing of the past. Families would clutch each other round the bathroom fire in that cozy but all too forgotten tradition of bored Himalayan monks who learned to the very quick how to crystal gaze at their fingernails. Of course they had to wait till the moons got full and it was this waiting that made the cynics very nervous, and so respond in kind with the more endearing, more enduring tradition of their own: Fingernail Biting. No doubt, to consume the evidence of mystics. At any rate, without oxymorons families would simply leave tv running at the mouth, and manifest. They would have a sticky tendency to make themselves mellow as a marsh, bobbing at prime rib time in a voluptuous bareheaded huddle, staring hypnotically at each other's toes, and sucking in, between nibbles, snowy lines of Robert Bly fondling frigid tree trunks and licking the Minnesota frogs. But this is not to be. As long as there are oxymorons there will be Minnesota frogs. Frogs that only yesterday were one day closer to their tadpole stage. When wet as tears and dropping as fast, they were little sweet sorrows in need of passing. As long as there are sweet sorrows in need of passing there will always be soap operas. As long as there are soap operas there will be tv. And as long as there is tv and a future to put it in, tv will go right on being a thing of the past. Instead of clutching each other, families will have only their own members to clutch. And oxymorons will continue to do little more for the gears of poetry than toss in a noncommittal banana, merely adding to the mesh. True, oxymorons can be powerful.

They may be cute as cuff links but they are, after all, your very own custom made bullseye voodoo pins with you for the doll. They are like mascara applied with a needle. You'll never look yourself in the eye again. You'll never look yourself again. That's why you'1l have to hang creativity on the hatrack or be prepared to sail it out the window while using this device. Oxymoron. Not hatrack or window which are, by the way, both devices. Nor do I mean needle in the eye which can produce highly creative results. Their magic (oxymorons, not creative results) is like the color of blood which changes when exposed to the air: they have a way of becoming obsolete immediately upon their discovery. They are probably why the discovery of blood, along with its discoverer, are at this very moment obsolete: "Blood! I'1l call it 'oodles'. Better yet, 'ketchup'! No. First we have to learn that tomatoes are edible. I know, I'11 call it 'life giving'." Not bad words to be forgotten by, especially when they're your last. But of course we have thick and sticky on our hands, the first oxymoron: life as we Icon it, and the idea of receiving a desirable gift, are such ridiculously incompatible contradictions (especially considering the gaping circumstances surrounding blood's discovery) that they cannot exist in the same breath without rendering it stale (breath, that is, not—well yeah, blood too). What if no one thought of "sounds of silence" till you did right this minute? Do you really think that would keep you from being dated with Simon and Garfunkle? "Intimate strangers" may refer to one night stands, rapists, overpopulated cemeteries, or the ensuing relationship between writer and reader. Does the point need demonstrating? Does it cast a bright shadow on your otherwise lunar eclipsed day? Does it make your circle rimless with lonely friendships? In fact, there may be conditions in which these descriptions can—but should not—apply. With the exception of "bright shadow" which never applies but should (We would all like to see one). But the end result might fit right in with your circle of lonely friendships. It's like the nose on your face: who wants to be plain? So if you answered yes to all of the above questions with the exception of the one about your nose, then you're absolutely right. The point does need demonstrating. In which case you just read the demonstration and still missed the point. In which case for you, the point does not need demonstrating. So in any case you're wrong. So in either case you're both right and wrong. You're inaccurately correct. Am I boring you? If not, it's doubtful you're worth the paper you read on. In fact, you're making me disgusting. But knowing you, you'll naively go right on reading this, following your nose for every nitpick of advice. Well, take this advice: stop reading. Stop writing. And start coloring in anatomy books. How I hate you. On the other hand, if you are bored, then you've stopped reading this anyway. I find that refreshing and liberating. Sticks and stones...but words, etc. I can write anything I want to now, because NO ONE IS READING (WAKEFUL SLEEP! SUFFOCATED BREATHING! PREGNANT EMPTINESS! BLIND VIEW!). And that's the point. If the only thing you follow is my example, then no one will read you either. And you too can be delivered from the bitchgoddess, Alphabet.

The point is, stick to the point and stop trying to be profound—or funny, being respectively the conscious and unconscious desire of oxymoronic minds. In the former case the writer thinks he has found a rare jewel of a tool. But in fact profundity isn't like a gold pickax at all. Like dumped chemicals, profundity is everywhere. Believe me, it's in every breath you take and discard. It can crush the strongest dixie cup. In fact, nothing is more commonplace than profundity. Does that statement amaze you? Then go into television news reporting. Or ghost write for Ripley's "Believe it or not".

**Of course the term, oxymoron, is itself an oxymoron. "Oxy" means sharp while "moron" is a person of very dull wits.*

en passant

passed three bag ladies today
and about a thousand grey brown and blue suits
passed me.
I'm so damned lucky.

A Recurring Nightmare

now that I am asleep
they can move to the other end of the house
and fight in peace…

the bit of my pillow
steers best bare
in this draftless heat
the shriveled friction on my bed sheets
rubs the pillow case
                                        off like a blister
                                        loose and wet
my crown cushion is skinned down
to domestic zebra
my pegasus striped with down.

tonight the feathers
the skin hunted fans
tonight they fly my face wet
and carry me down the fertile river humps
and carry the air tripping hooves
and carry my feet above them, clinched
without the trappings
carry the fancy striped
                                        fringe of mane
the ox like tail
that wags up like a warning forefinger
and farts like a jet

I will ride this tune's old familiar wave
that carries me down somewhere in Egypt
down to the rivers
down to the tombs
down to the sand-
                              anchored ribs and the scrambled
riderless vertebrae
down random alphabet blocks

the child's play of death scaling
down the twisted heads

of hunched hyenas high in the tooth
high in the neck
low in the forever grin.
there is no more Egypt
no undiscovered, unwrapped nest
no more pillow to wink from
there are no pitying tooth traders hovering
slight as American humming birds
above petal soft yawning lips
or hiving between them like flies
for their treasure,
there are no tooth fairies
there are only flies.
the zebra meat is flat

but what's high is the calliope piston neck
of horseylike head twisted
                    high
                              the forever frown
                              drilled completely around
                              the carousel animal's bit

as if in the flesh, that hiatus in the gums
was born to no other purpose
than to harbor and tongue the bit placed there,
driven there by the hands of a master

but in the beast of painted wood (the effigy of
                                                  dreams),
it takes a mechanical drill to drive
an impaling barber pole of steel
                              bit guided firm
                              in the hands of a master

in the hands of a master

the bore of a bullet
could pull the teeth of elephants

unsheathe their ivory crescents
two by two
and carve the curve of scimitars
again, with the hands of a master.
how many masters' hands does it take?

till I'm big enough I won't have to cry
myself to sleep anymore
and be the only big boy in the night
and snore loud as I please with the haunt
of elephant's nose sensitive as snake
                                        or snake tongue
                                exploring, tactile, restless,
                                lover of mates and trees
                                winding, unwinding...

and down, on down where unrewarded
temple vipers guard to the double hilt
but survive the shed of hunted skin

there is no more temple
no treasure to outgrow
no more pillow to wink from
there is only habit

that guards, it still guards
my face downward
to the pillow's soft, impotent bite

against the precious skull corridors
against the bare back's bucking heap
of wind ribboned sand
a rib boned finger
-fold of soil shimmering black and white
between the horny blows of time's

hit and miss.
spine and spineless.

Dear death carousel,
to ride your zebra
whiplashing stripes
to bow and kiss your crewcut stubble
(tears on your neck
are so much sweat on the piston shank)
there are feathers inside of you
my spanked hollow piñata,
that fly to the fist
one too many times
and that is how often I wake
from your pumping wings…

my mother cannot be rib to him
there are hit and miss welts
on the backs of my legs (his little piñata)
from what she cannot be to him
I am survived by the shed of hunted skin
and now that I am old enough to ride
the same nightmare over and over
finally that old,
in the hands of a master
I hold the strap to him
the razor strap that normally hones the blade
foaming
white on stiff black stubble
zebra mane impaled
by Merry-Go-Round
barber pole—unmanly,
my palm slime passes
so much sweat on so much piston shank
I make the greasy adjustments
red and white now,
red and white
I ride him to his death and still I ride him

Giddyup Daddy
Giddyup

Pretend Children's Poems

Number Poem

I have a kite
with almost all
the paper off
and it doesn't have
a tail
but I don't think
it would fly anyway
cause it's really the
number
four
and numbers can get
awfully heavy.

Get Small Poem

if I could get around
like a fly
upside down
under my desk
I would find
a petrified forest
of gum.

and I'd be glad
it's petrified!

When Hands are Toys

beneath a steeple preschool children
spawn out thumb doors
under a forefingers steeple.
today it is not polite to point
even up.

in obedient play
two forefingers lean against each other
a kind of forced kiss
while all the other fingers cleverly enmesh
and fold under
obscured
by sentry thumbs
they are right about that part
thumbs are gates

and when they open
fingers wiggle like snotty worms
to get out

Ransom Uncollected for a Pigeon's Feather

wing of your wing
you do not miss
dipped in your flesh
skywritten
so many times dipped
in the air
your air, your
unflattened memory

returning
a swim of breezes
naked
to the touch
are they the real
carriers of messages
you do not miss?

To a Dying Pigeon

I.

It is not oil that speckles the sidewalk
when like a toy winding down
one wing plays the axis
to the other's beating rounds

now as always
I watch for your complaints
(a respect for soft graffiti)
but this time hobbled

in the lap continuously
out of shape as if inside
something is dark and tilted to push button
flippers, the wings of pinball's

sin-raked gutters to now
as always you mock
deliverance
was it anything like this

the day you first sat
on telegraph wire?
what more would it have taken to get the message
your messenger days were numbered!

When you retired from the service
and moved to the city
when we could see you
out-squatting the sun all day long

see the glint
of purple heart on your breast
was there not even a memory's itch
round your leg? A cast

of thousands the signatures
you've carried
but now there is no one
including myself

either to unscroll or to wrap
the fist-tight core of your lameness
and only yourself to shake the memories
the goodbyes in you returning

something inside your head
reasonable as broken covenants
metallic rainbows wring your neck
déjà vu from the oil slick noons?

A closer look
where mere looks and closeness invade.
your dodging target-flat eyes
tell me nothing

why does that surprise me?

II.

If your skull were big enough
I would simply divide your brain like
a Victorian bed board
and try to experiment with what you really
had in mind
as "Home"

then, with you too drunk on your blood
I would take you there
(if I am not standing on the very spot!)
if your skull were big enough I would hang

harness

and reins on you. I would hang on you pennies
for blinders and take you there
you giving directions through dead
sold out eyes

what unseen freedom flapped through them
that has left you so very smooth
so very limp
so very very soft?

Not now as you give your cloak back
but when you first shook claws with man?
Art, beauty, death and freedom—-all of it—all
at what risk our own infectious debris extends

a Michelangelo touch
to nature
near-death placing the wild
near benevolence?

You who know the statues
you who mistake them
for your glory
you who know what we mistake

for heaven
have you taken in
Sistine Chapel's Ceiling?
Are there wings

between Adam's pushbutton death of God?
Forgive me
we are too close for words
and I am too late

to spark in us the distance

they held for each other
the distance
their painter's hand still holds

for his creator
for his creation
for me
still we comply

the same goodness
in our goodness:
Victim. Rescuer.
I know no other

from our common shelter's lining
that cranes the neck
that drips a rainbow's oil
that speckles

the beard of artist
ruler, whoever happens to lie
beneath…or above
between us

we manage the whole of good
in the universe!
Alone you could spoil
in the highest of places

with your blood. Commissioned
of images and parables, spoil
the tomb of Pope Julius, The Second
carry his kidnapper's loyalty

on to Michelangelo. You, The Franciscan
blade as a wing. Your flight
a sword to the Venetians
a masquerade as a dove

with your blood. And I who hold you
like a fingerprinted weapon waiting
till the traces worry me
to guilt

and wondering if Julius, general on the field
didn't ask, and wondering if Michelangelo
didn't ask: Are they dreams alone that tug
the wing against the wing

repeatedly in battle
                    or prayer
                    or art
                    or death

or whatever grips at one wing of a
                              wound toy beating
repeatedly
like a kite
till at last the movement stops

when in my hand?

Pretend Children's Poems

Seed Poem

Maple Wing Baby
you got trapped
inside and someone's
stepped on you
and now you're too hungry
to cry.
I've seen broken
dolls in better shape
but that's OK.
you can play with me.
I'll take you far
above your head
and let you go.
but I think for you
the party's over.
you stick your weak
finger in the air
and just go
w
e
e
e
e
e
e
e
e
e

The 1987 Cent

I stack them
whenever I read over breakfast
confusion between our president the actor
and our actor the president
the heads and tails, I stack them

in remembrance of pancakes just devoured
these pennies not honeyed over
Universal pennies, these
inedible anywhere
under brazen foot
on the coffee counter
these pennies
I think not skillet-scraped from the patina

of our Miss Liberty's scoured-new image
in the same stance of Her birth
How defiant! To never know foetal
chest humbled on foetal knees
to have never gathered in

folded body with the nascent hug of arms
and how brazen!
Risqué you would think
but sexlessly She extends
a single sandal's exposure
that cheats the hem of Her toga
as if still acting right up to under the curtain's

fall
but then spies a quarter on the stage floor
directs attention to above
and claims it with Her foot!

In my boyhood I picked up Dairy Queen trash
I would trap from the wind with the ball of my

foot

I got a quarter a day
and saved what I got, you'd think I was out to buy
a pony, I would never waste them
on milkshakes like my brother
but hoarded
counted
each new quarter
made me count them all over again
I knew every one of them
every smudge every rubbed-down relief of their
faces
they didn't look all alike to me
if one was missing I knew it
they were my sheep through the gate

One day I opened a bank account
from all those coins and they were like children
grown up, off to college, and too heavy to spank
a couple hundred dollars passed through the gate

Then Easter
when my brother and I got our perennial
chocolate eggs
Gary would decimate his
Mine stayed in the refrigerator for days
two weeks maybe
I nibbled.
Chocolate was rare and dark as the best soil
you could dig Jumbo worms in
I nibbled and stored like some killer cottontail
Gary grew up rich and successful

Government grants for science, medicine and all
he's probably president by now
of his prosthetic implant company
I am an amateur artist who didn't grow up
decreased, in fact

got nibbled and stored away
much closer to actor than president, I
decided to treat money symbolically
and only symbolically
treat it like things. Like words.
Talking heads at the most.
From then on I'll save any penny I see on the
sidewalk
call it lucky
treat it as if it was thrown at me
on some spotlit stage
treat it with respect

There are times if I buy anything
even food
it's only an act

But these pennies
I stack on the counter now
I leave them for you, Louise
waitress of the not mutually exchanged
first names
I like to get rid of them on tips anyway
you know by now my tips are high enough
to expiate me if I happen to linger
read, write, and expect
an artesian of nerves out of my beggar's coffee
cup—these pennies

you take them, Louise
hoard them like a marsupial in your apron
these pennies make up exactly 20% of pancakes
egg
and coffee
no more

These pennies
showing duplicate Lincoln-heads

on the face-down tab should tell you
dear waitress and public servant, I too
am an American capable
of taxes accumulated for the country's
debt
neglect of families of the chocolate soil
not to mention brother
against brother
war against civil
slavery
not to mention fatal wounds to the head
dear waitress, a Lincoln-head penny
for your thoughts, if it is only the head
history draws a bead on
whenever there is bulls-eye confusion
between actor
and president

To Be Played

with an increasing faltering sense
of purpose
movements
aimlessly alto
like *castrati* afterthoughts derailing
with a vengeance (or, if you must,
falsetto. but still)
not forgetting nostalgia's
little stabs at happiness
from a distance

Though I Can't Feel Them

just below my window
midst alarmingly patient
snow flakes' feathery settling
on any target not moving,
on thick fork of two limbs
where their greyness swells
two turtle doves
tufted in their streamlines
twinned by the sculpturing cold
portrait-still, unfreezing
models indistinguishable
from each other or from
some refined carver's equivalent
for the privileged eye
to share this intimate
one same tuck
blended stark-still
easily mistaken
as if from the finest sandpaper-rub of sea
smooth as a driftwood knot

Round Nihilism

In the beginning there were I don't know
how many makers of brick
each one used a fiddle
to pat the clay mud down in the mold
(fiddle or some other tribal weapon
in those days they didn't respect instruments)
and they did this to drums but what kind
I don't remember
they didn't beat in unison anyway

but that didn't keep everyone from dancing
all danced to the meter of the masons
the wrist-flick
                    slop of mortar

dance, the Miltonian cathedral walls of music
          built on pandemonium
chaos, the echo
                    of ribs
                              vaulting inside and
out, hilarious flying buttresses'
stoic skeleton dance
                              holding holding
irrelevant to the air
breathing beneath

Problem was you couldn't see
what they embraced
                              in the slow numbers.
Every rib has to have a partner
to get up and move with.
Any First Man could tell you that.
But the ballad shuffle
lagged so it all looked like standing.
They took the time of skeletons
with the slow numbers

and built standing room only
in the old colossal shindig Chartres
or Notre Dame and besides, the fancy glass
                                        juke box Mass
needed some light
        behind the punch-drunk push buttons
and that's where the sun came in

Problem was
stained glass isn't an economical
way of looking at the sun
but then, neither is
looking at the sun.

Try that
and the only way you'll ever read time
is feel the light come through
like hot glass buttons on blind fingers
you'd have to memorize what order the windows
fasten the walls

so they all just sat shadeless
in the stone and mud with knees folded
to wait like brick worshipers
for the sun to harden

harden intransitive
all that accumulated patience
turned the sun's own furnace into a ceramic orb!
So now they had their demolition ball
to paste on mosaic of busted up mirror
                        from condemned windows
now the sun was a spinning
jigsaw-of-squares demolition ball
to shine the spotlight on
                        and keep the stars dancing

        pointed no matter how high the angle

it's still stained glass
tinted as autumn and just as broken
where parables are born
by our kaleidoscope squint
fallen

like the sperm of Holy Spirit
in the Mother Virgin's
ear
—that tunnel to the drum
—that beating window
parables conceived and seen
in their rightful splinters

it was ball of shine
and spangle from flapper to disco, I tell you
till now they had demolition swing

to roll up their sleeves to, and pull
on the kicking and screaming dance
like Shiva on the birth
like urban renewal

I don't think you quite get the picture
how from any angle
how symmetric light like that is
all the turning in the world
isn't going to change
the symmetry, the gravity
kaleidoscopes worship

the gravel flung
mortar of gravity
on wrecking ball
its dance ball
swing of gravity
that says what heel-pivot foot goes up
comes down

in time

the gravity that makes a whole highrise city
wait for the fall of night
                before there's enough light see
it had spent all the day
long in celebration, really:
        sun's high or low
                            brow
                                  sweat falls,
                            always celebrates
        so much sperm to the ground's ear
                always out of control
                        falling
                        celebrating

the gravity that spends the rest of the night
celebrating that

                        on through the final hours
till humid, nocturnal
                instruments get worn down
                like claws on cement
                and by the window-cast
                                        brick of dawn
        get forgotten with the beat that some say
wasn't in unison
                anyway

Lesson

if you're eating a great meal
from a paper bag,
with five minutes to go
before the bell,
you're not eating
a great
meal

—from a radio talk show conversation

BOARD COLLABORATION #1

Flying
at least they said it was
but the sky was hard
and the day was full
of pennies & hair
squeaking bats in the night
Flying.

BOARD COLLABORATION #2

Farewell the plasma!
The secret's in silk-wrapped eyes
of the spiders
singing, spinning
the joy in and out
of a depthness:
jar of peanut butter.
I dreamed I was the spider
but who am I to believe in dreams?
Perhaps the plastic
plants—permanently
healthy.

BOARD COLLABORATION #3

The wind whispers it to the grass
Mandrake holds it in his secret root
Snakes thicken & swell to the thought
Of music wrapped in lusty rhythms
in the orange grove
of breasts singing
on a frozen pond
and we have lost
our leader, broken down.

BOARD COLLABORATION #4

Nothing will ever be the same
The only thing which changes
        is the thing that remains the same
Darting tongues & pulling lips
What goes around, comes around
"Jason, ain't you shamed a' you self?"
"No, no I jus' don' wanna be the bait, no, no,
        Uncle Bill"
And the Eagle will rise again
into primordial essence
or a worn black G-string.

BOARD COLLABORATION #5

Ashes spin to flame in my room
Born again in spring
Wild breezes flutter within
Strong winds intimidate this valley
But winds of Phoenix fan & warm the world
And I want to fall.......asleep
My spirit freed to live and try again
Whipped up and fanned just above the rocks
It hangs, a silvery disc luminous on the horizon.

BOARD COLLABORATION #6

I gaze upon a higher light
A mist gown shimmering silver
Fog enshrouds a streetlamp at the alley's end
here, where I have always been
a stranger.

BOARD COLLABORATION #8*

There are daggers of wheat
        hidden in the bread
and semi-colons like lettuce
slip inside my tongue
dirty sombreros tilt listlessly
        over whole tamales
high noon & shadows
release these things to lacerate
                my head
as a question marks my gut
the dagger's in the sand

**Board Collaboration #7 was not found among Rudy's papers*

You Wait

On This Vigilant Eve Commemorating the Twentieth Century Holocaust of the Jews

You just wait and all the trains
for glory are going to snake
through the land like god-rivers
skimming a race what drinks the desert
keeps the memory orphaned
from that first crossing
whichever it was The Exodus
before The Exodus:
seems more than once this leaving and holding
the first a cradle
of reeds floating
if bottle tight is your Moses
hope getting carried away your Yiddish
tongues spilt over
and over and on and off the tracks
again stitching throughout the countryside
your cargo packed
tight as fish roe, your seed's
burden thrusting clay
a humus rising
skimmed papless off the alluvial current
irreversible
a rocking
a putting to sleep.
It is an alien cradle
it is infertile ark

that stays upright
at best gets grounded
stranded.
Designed for that!
And waits.
Waits for the dove bitten
olive branch and waits

for the rain soaked rainbow
and waits for the nearest island
of mountain peak.
You remain
as one
proud finicky
beggar when out of the wilderness
only one Coming will do
but didn't.

When rails bound for glory crossed
themselves over
and over from head
to heart, crossed
like trampled ladders anchored,
trammeled to the earth
and alien homes and cradles bound
to the glory of eagles spanned
high over The Fatherland
linked their iron fists
from boxcar to boxcar
as if the world would never wait
for these trains to pass
but did.

It is a windowless passage
hitching the spines of the land:
Forgetting,
Forgotten.
Infertile
the ark that has to be left
is going to be left forever
one of a kind.

Pretend Children's Poems

Things I collect

I collect pieces of things.
the rule is nothing can be completely what it is.
it can be new, but it can't be complete.
my dad says these days that's not so hard

But you have to be able to tell
by looking at it that something's missing.
you may know what's missing and you may not
but still you can tell by looking at it
it's just not all there.

I have a brass horse
and a leg's gone and it can still stand up
just because it broke its leg doesn't mean
I gotta kill it

And 'course there are broken things
you play with, but that's too easy.
so I collect old broken things
that no one plays with anymore

I have a yoyo half
and an old electric football game
with beebee dents in it
and no players

And I put pieces of chat on it
and watch them vibrate
around and in the bee-bee dents
and that's how I play
with things you don't play with anymore

Doesn't

a self portrait

He doesn't see the light shafting down the top
of his head
He doesn't donate his eyes or his kidneys
He doesn't mail the tips of his fingers to his
friends
the ones he can count on
He doesn't know how to forget that surfaces
demand to be looked at
He doesn't know how to let a woman know
he's looking at her
He doesn't know how to do anything that
can't be observed
He doesn't mind being cut off
so long as he doesn't know about it till later
He doesn't see the light flickering out
through the top of his head
he doesn't have to

In Remembrance of Rudy Jon Tanner

by Richard Loranger and Deborah L. Fruchey

In the same week that the Bay Area lost Jack Hirschman, we also lost poet Rudy Jon Tanner, a gentleman and gentle man who had been on the scene for over forty years. Rudy was born in 1946 in Oklahoma, where he originally played cello and aspired to work in a symphony orchestra. He studied 20th Century Composition at Oklahoma City University, where he began writing poetry. He also briefly served in the military.

Rudy came to the Bay Area in 1980, and was soon a regular at the Spaghetti Factory readings in North Beach. There he met Julia Vinograd, who was to be his friend for the rest of her life. Between 1980 and 2000, he published two chapbooks: the former under the auspices of Paul Landry entitled *Picasso's Monkey*, followed by one from Deep Forest Press, *The Accidental Beacons of Things Worn Away*. The title poem of the latter became his best-known piece.

Rudy suffered from a number of health conditions which made it difficult for him to support himself. He was born with a rare genetic disorder, and also suffered from depression and fierce environmental allergies which made it impossible for him to live or work anywhere near fresh paint or carpet. In his later years, he developed lymphoma, which proved to be terminal, and severely limited his activities. But he was a kind man, and reserved, and few knew of all these conditions.

Rudy's cautious and reclusive lifestyle, coupled with his astute mental capacity, led him to become a fierce observer. His poetry often evokes intricate webs of details, histories, interconnections, mutualities. Human relations are especially resonant in his work, perhaps his way of reaching out emotionally beyond his limited means. The poem "The Accidental Beacons of Things Worn Away", for instance, focuses on a close examination of his grandfather's shaving cup, from which unfold intergenerational linkages and tragedies, an ongoing father-to-son lineage which is both archetypical and acutely personal. We arrive back to the speaker, Rudy, holding the cup and wondering exactly how much we can know of each other, and how much we can't.

Rudy also became skilled in origami, and gifted his friends with intricate folded Christmas ornaments and handmade envelopes. He played piano on Sundays for the Spiritualist Church of Two Worlds in San Leandro, carrying his electric piano with him. He wrote one of their favorite hymns, which they sang at his memorial.

Around the year 2000, Rudy at last applied for and received Disability, and was able to move into his own one-bedroom apartment in Oakland. He devoted himself to composition for his remaining years. At one point his brilliant piece for two pianos, the intersection of which make a third distinct song, was sought for use in film ('spare no expense' was the phrase used); but he was already too ill to pursue the opportunity. He gave rare piano performances, once splitting audience time with Julia Vinograd, at her request. Julia wrote a tribute poem for his music titled "Climbing Lightning," which can be found in her book *When Even the Sky Hurts*.

In 2020 he was delighted by the publication of his full-length poetry collection *If Thirst is Proof of Water* by Zeitgeist Press.

Rudy died quietly in his apartment on August 19, 2021, at the age of 75. He is survived by his older brother, Gary Tanner, and leaves behind a wealth of poetry and song.

Climbing the Lightning

for Rudy Jon Tanner's Music

A piano climbing the lightning,
        the fiercely human lightning.

Job's whirlwind opposed to God's whirlwind:
a mortal fury of dead babies
crying from bathsoap in their eyes,
blessings gone bad as overripe rotting peaches
and unforgivably, love. Still love.
Ghosts of ruthless mountains walk the low notes
throwing sunsets over cliffs
until they crash like winebottles.
Each pause precedes a Hitchcock murder
and a Virgin birth, superimposed.
His hands look down on the high notes.

Not just music, it's a savage gymnasium
for muscles of the mind, lifting storms,
bending the eye like Superman bends
        steel prison bars.
Music making trouble, a discord of wild light
shedding the world like a rippling snakeskin
all new underneath.

Julia Vinograd
from *When Even the Sky Hurts*
(Zeitgeist Press, 2010)

Other Books by This Author:

Chapbooks

Picasso's Monkey
(Paul Landry)

The Accidental Beacons of Things Worn Away
(Deep Forest Press)

Full Length Books

If Thirst is Proof of Water
(Zeitgeist Press, 2020)

For Whoever Thinks a Piano is Furniture
(Last Laugh Productions, 2023)

"If Thirst is Proof of Water"
is available from ZeitgeistPress.com.
All other books are available at this publisher, except
"Picasso's Monkey", which is sadly out of print.
Contact lastlaughpro@gmail.com
for copies.

Other Books from Last Laugh Productions

The Hall of Painted Sonnets

by Steve Arntson & Diane Lee Moomey

Gypsy & Other Poems

by Steve Arntson

Armageddon Bootcamp

by Maria Elizabeth Rosales

Priestess of Secrets

by Deborah L. Fruchey

Touchstones

by Maria Elizabeth Rosales

Bat Flower:

poems, plays & other perversions

by Vampyre Mike Kassel

Mental Illness Ain't for Sissies

by Deborah L. Fruchey

www.lastlaughproductions.org

www.ingramcontent.com/pod-product-compliance
Lightning Source LLC
Chambersburg PA
CBHW061241170626
46809CB00007B/2779

* 9 7 9 8 9 8 7 5 2 0 9 1 8 *